A
SHAMANIC
ALTAR

A
SHAMANIC
ALTAR

Recollections of Thirty Years of Shamanic Practice

Philip Dana Robinson

EWH Press

MICHIGAN, 2015

Published by EWH Press
PO Box 537
Leslie, MI 49251
www.ewhpress.com

ISBN 978-0-9903500-5-7
EWH Press first printing, February 2015

Cover and book design by Terrie MacNicol
Edited by Jeff Stoner

Printed in the United States of America

Dedication:

To Shana and Rocky with all of my Love

ACKNOWLEDGMENTS

A Shamanic Altar was made possible only with the help of the Spirits who have supported me even when I was unaware of their existence. There are times, I am certain, when they literally saved my life.

My wife Shana's patience with me, encouragement and constant nurturing are the true measure of wealth. She is the center of our home, and I gladly fill the role of planet circling around the bright star that she is. A man must know his place.

I owe so much to Michael Harner and his Foundation for Shamanic Studies. He gave me the keys to the kingdom and gave me the opportunity to share the exquisite spirit worlds and their inhabitants with others. I cherish my friendship with him and his beautiful wife Sandra.

Many thanks to the students I have had the honor to teach and from whom I have learned much. Their intelligence, sensitivity, enthusiasm and courage give me hope for the human race.

In part, this book is an ode to the life forms of our great planet. I pledge my eternal love and loyalty to the animals and plants of Earth as well as to its oceans, rivers, mountains, forests, deserts; to my home, the Blue Planet, on the edge of the Milky Way Galaxy.

There are so many who have enriched my life through their companionship, their joy, artistry, wisdom, and humor. Many have never heard of me. I hope that some of what they have given to me can be found in the following pages. Here is a short list: my parents, Rudy Bauer, Harold Goodman, Bob Smith, Trish Raley, Lee Ritenour, Govinda Singh, Pastor Richard Klein, Marian Starnes, Patrick McGoohan, Paul Craig Roberts, and several hundred other wonderful people, some of whom appear later in this book.

The support of my publishers, Jeff Stoner and Terrie MacNicol, has been priceless. Without their expert help, this book would not exist.

Allow me to express my gratitude to you, dear reader. I hope that you find this short work inspiring.

CONTENTS

INTRODUCTION

I do not call myself a shaman. I am just a man who goes to the great compassionate spirits seeking healing and advice for others and myself. These words echo those of Grandfather Duvan, of the Ulchi ethnic group (from far eastern Siberia), who was 94 years old when we spent five days with him in the mid-1990s in Northern California. This was a man who was recognized by his tribe as a shaman and had been practicing shamanism for seventy-five years or more. We learned many things from Grandfather, not the least of which was the beauty of authentic humility. My teacher, Michael Harner, the man who brought shamanism to the modern West and a special purpose to my life, has said that no one in their right mind calls himself a shaman; let those who are helped shamanically determine who is and who is not worthy of the title.

What is a shaman? Harner, in *Cave and Cosmos*, the excellent and long-awaited follow-up to his classic *The Way of the Shaman*, has expanded the definition to include those who utilize an altered state of consciousness to "engage in purposeful two-way interaction with spirits." The shaman typically takes shamanic journeys, that is, spirit voyages to the realms outside of time and physical space called, amongst other things, the Upper World and the Lower World; the journey is undertaken to help the living as well as the deceased. The shaman, on occasion, embodies the helping spirits upon which he relies. No wonder it is said that the first actors on the planet were the shamans, engaged, possibly, in the purest form of method acting. The shaman sublimates his own personality giving his being over to the personality and power of one of his Spirit Allies. The word shaman comes from the Tungus people of Siberia and translated means he or she who knows. As one begins to experientially study shamanism, as one works directly with the great compassionate spirits, what the shaman knows becomes clearer and clearer.

Shamanism is a great spiritual adventure, probably the first spiritual practice of humanity, dating to the times of the earliest cave art, 40,000 years ago (the Cave of El Castillo in Spain, Kakadu in Australia) and earlier. It originated in a time when people most assuredly had a better sense of their place in the natural world, when non-human species were considered sacred, long before the emergence of the human-centered organized religions of today which have promoted so much destruction and death. Shamanism is a path to self-knowledge, to becoming healed and to becoming a healer. It is a gateway to the realms of exquisite beauty that lie beyond the physical world. It offers us a return to the innocent wonder of childhood and is a bridge to our ancestors, some of whom were practicing shamanism.

I have taught over 600 weekend shamanism workshops over the last twenty-eight years. Each morning of a workshop, I lay out my altar in the center of the conference room. I have observed other teachers simply place a candle in the center of the workshop space. I began with a candle and later added a small Native American blanket and various items that are particularly meaningful for me, some of which were gifts. I store them on the inside of my drum, which I place inside of a drum bag, when I'm not using them. There are stories associated with most of the items which I share in this book in order to pass along the teachings that they represent. For me, my altar is my 'medicine bundle' laid out—my collection of sacred objects which embody power themselves and remind me of significant spiritual events. This book is devoted to one specific altar utilized in shamanic work.

1 | A Shamanic Altar

My altar is a small Native American rug, upon which rest various items of spiritual, highly personal, emotional and historical significance, most of which are symbolic of stories. As I lay out the altar and place each item on the rug, I try to remember the item's significance. These gestures and thoughts help me prepare to serve as a facilitator for workshop participants as they swim in the altered state seas of the spirit worlds, as they come face to face with the wise and compassionate spirits that await discovery and an opportunity to help.

Laying out the altar is an invitation to the spirits represented to grace us with their presence. One could have a permanent altar at home or in one's garden or some other special and appropriate spot. I enjoy setting up my altar in the center of our meeting circle and putting it to rest at the end of the day; this activity promotes the focus I will need to have to lead a workshop. I feel that the freshness of the altar is maintained through putting it to rest at the end of day.

Fire is the focal point of the altar. The flame is alive. It is symbolic of the light of the universe, the stars. We, along with everything else, are children of the stars, which created all elements beyond hydrogen and helium. The Big Bang created those two fundamental elements, and so we are also children of the Big Bang. The flame is a reminder of the fire that burns within each living creature. Those fires pale in size to the enormous fires of the stars and the incomprehensible fire of the Big Bang, and yet, is the fire that burns within the body of the ant or the amoeba or the eagle or the whale any less miraculous? We are at once consoled by the flame and humbled by it.

Humans, in general, have lost their connection with all that is, with the plants, animals, rocks, waters, etc. Observe the earliest cave paintings. They depict animals. Their ultimate purpose may be debatable, but the reverence for animals is clearly conveyed. Many thousands of years pass before humans are featured in pictographs and petroglyphs. As we have become more human-centered, we have become more alienated from the exquisite world around us. This has made possible the pollution of our planet, the mass murder of various creatures including whales, buffalo, sharks, dolphins, bears, elephants, and birds, and a thousand other transgressions. One wonders if the human race is mimicking the lemmings' march to the sea, making certain in that death march that numerous other species are annihilated along the way.

The shamanic altar, with representations of some of earth's creatures who hold a special place for the altar's owner, is a way to reconnect with our four-legged, winged, or scaly brothers and sisters who, although they wear different skins, are at least our equals. Equals? Just for starters, these creatures are able to survive, flourish actually, in the wild twenty-four hours a day, every day. How many humans are able to do that?

The altar reminds us that we have these connections. Some of the animals represented on the shamanic altar are animal spirit helpers; these beings embody spiritual power, which I define as intelligence plus energy plus ethics plus love. They are critical in the life and work of the shaman, who is well aware of the identity of these helpers. Have you noticed that whom you choose to associate with can have a profound influence upon you? Associating with beings embodying these qualities, which is what shamans who work in the Lower and Upper Worlds do, tends to make one a better person. There is something of an alchemical change in the person seriously engaged in shamanism. The shaman realizes that he is an emissary of the great helping spirits and his actions reflect upon those spirits. The shaman walks with the confidence of knowing that he has tremendous support; his "back is covered" and he can focus on what lies before him, on what needs to be said and what needs to be done.

Merging is one of the basic activities of the shaman; that is, becoming one with helping spirits either when the need arises or as part of a regular spiritual practice. These spirits are called into the shaman's physical body. There is a saying, "If you call them, they will come." Through this sort of merging, one brings into his body the power of these spirits; intelligence, energy, ethics and love enter the body of the practitioner and tend to remain, particularly when merging is practiced on a regular basis. Hence, the practitioner becomes an improved version of his former self.

Humans are copycats. Consciously or unconsciously we imitate others. Young boys worship sports heroes. Grown men and women look to Hollywood stars for cues in appearance and behavior. Our culture teaches us that most of us are not good enough, that we can't compete with the "great ones." The shaman, in merging with helping spirits, does not imitate but in fact becomes, for a time, those spirits, those great ones. There is plenty of incentive for merging: to be fused with power is pleasurable; one has the sense of being greater, of having a beautiful body and consciousness added to one's own being; one feels protected from illness, accidents, and bad luck. After the spirit fades out of the shaman's body, there remains a residue of power. Through constant merging and connecting, the shaman creates layer upon layer of power. Given the ingredients of this power, it can only be used in the most positive sort of way. Any attempt to use spiritual means in a negative way neutralizes the power which results in a loss of power. The helping spirits withdraw their support; the results can be cataclysmic.

According to Brian Bates in *The Way of the Actor*, the first actors on our planet were the shamans: "All so-called 'primitive' societies have at their head important people with special powers. These people have the ability to transform themselves in public performance from their normal personality into somebody or something else: a god or animal, ancient ancestor or representation of a spirit." Actually, the shaman calls upon a helping spirit and allows the spirit to blend with the shaman and express himself/itself through the shaman. The shaman is the hollow bone through which the spirits can act upon the world. The altar can be an initial point of the merging process as it is a reminder of the spirits available to be summoned. It is important to remember that the spirits are autonomous and their willingness to appear and cooperate is never to be taken for granted.

Denise Linn, in her book *Altars*, quotes Susan Torre, "The altar objects exert a powerful influence on the subconscious because they simultaneously express various levels of truth beyond the reality of surface appearances, thus helping to create understanding out of the complexities of life." The altar is a sacred space, mirroring, finally, our planet and the entire physical and spiritual universe. It is the microcosm reflecting the macrocosm. It is a representation of aspects of a perfect world, and it provides a target toward which we can aim our lives. Still, this is the pursuit not of perfection but of goodness. Setting up the altar and reflecting upon it transforms it into a kind of magnet which draws us toward the ideal world which it symbolizes. In addition, the objects of the altar draw toward them the beings that they represent.

As we gaze upon the altar objects and even *through* them, we are reminded that the world represented is not unattainable but in fact is as close as the altar is to us. The unseen world of spirits is just a drumbeat away from being directly perceived. The spiritual resides but a quantum step beyond the physical. Perhaps human goodness resides just as close beyond human destructiveness.

2 | THE CANDLE & WOLF

The central piece of my altar is the candle, which sits on a colored glass concave dish atop a three-prong glass stand reminiscent of the standing stones at sacred circles in Great Britain. My own ancestors from England and Wales may have contributed to their construction. The lit candle is representative of the light of our sun and all of the stars of the physical universe. Ancient peoples, most notably the Egyptians, worshipped the sun. Surely, our sun deserves to be honored by contemporary people on a daily basis. It is the center of our solar system and holds that system together. It lights our days and provides the warmth required to sustain life. It fuels Earth's plants which feed, directly or indirectly, almost all other life forms on our planet. Our bodies are comprised of and dependent upon many elements beyond hydrogen and helium, the two elements formed early in the birth of our universe. The heavier elements were forged in the centers of stars and in the supernova explosions of stars. Thus, we and all life forms are truly children of the suns. In lighting the candle, we recognize the place of the stars and their light in our lives.

Below the flame I have placed two medallions, one displaying the wolf, the other the bear, in the artistic style of the Northwest Coast First Peoples. More about the bear in a subsequent chapter. The wolf reminds me of some events that took place in 1993 on a small island in the 1,700 island coral reef archipelago known as the Florida Keys. I had been asked to teach a workshop to a small group by the no longer extant Keys Institute. The setting was a tiny key (island) with a main house once owned by the actor Dan Blocker (of the TV series *Bonanza*) and a caretaker's house. To get to the island, workshop participants met on a Thursday afternoon at the lush, manicured Ocean Reef Club, the home of the rich and famous, located at a secluded corner of Key Largo, Florida. The Keys are tropical nature on steroids. Mangroves are a foundation of their ecosystem and are breeding grounds for many forms of aquatic life and serve as rookeries and homes for birds such as pelicans, egrets and spoonbills. American crocodiles, bald eagles and rattlesnakes find shelter in these green blankets covering salt water beds. The waters of the keys are myriad shades of blue and green.

Our group boarded a forty-foot cabin cruiser which motored toward the workshop site fifty minutes away. It is a characteristic of our shamanic trainings that participants tend to get to know one another quickly. I soon learned that a particularly impressive woman onboard, Jane, had huddled the year before with her family in the interior of her home as Hurricane Andrew completely destroyed their house. Hurricanes and violent tropical storms are an integral part of the Keys, and Andrew was one of the costliest hurricanes in U.S. history. After the storm, Jane and her family relocated to Jupiter, FL, which suffered through Hurricane Wilma's Category 3 winds in 2005. Another workshop participant was a particularly likeable man who would later become world famous for his books on the darker side of third world development.

Our Florida key was a far more exotic location than I was accustomed to. My usual venues included school gyms, a lower Manhattan dance studio, American Legion posts infused with the odors of booze, and hotel conference rooms. After some down time and dinner, we began the training. With my rattle, I called in the helping spirits from the six directions using a ritual given to me by the spirit of an Amazonian Indian whom I met on a shamanic journey to the Upper World. Afterwards, the group briefly discussed the aliveness and intelligence awash in our world, embodied by the plants and animals of the great water planet, Earth. The piercing sound of a bird, somewhere out in the liquid night, silenced us for a moment; it seemed that the world had heard us and was agreeing with us.

While my workshops usually begin on Saturday morning and end on late Sunday afternoon, this one was unique, running from Thursday evening to noon on Sunday. We had time to do something beyond the regular curriculum. I have always loved dogs and have been enchanted by their progenitors, the wolves. The moon was close to being full on Saturday evening. It occurred to me that this was the perfect time for a one-off activity: our group would experience the wolf as perhaps none of us ever had before. I explained what I had in mind and our participants all agreed to participate.

We marched out of the house at 9pm into the tropical night alight in the shimmering reflected rays of the moon. We were pierced by the moon's silver slivers of light. And yet the darkness was intense since we were far from any artificial light. We stopped at a clearing near the water. I asked the group to look at the moon and call on the spirit of the wolf to join us, each person open to being merged with by a wolf spirit. I encouraged the participants to allow the wolf to vocalize through their voices, should they sense that imperative. Within a few minutes, most people, clearly merged with the wolf, were howling. This continued for a few minutes and ended when I beat on my drum, the signal to end the activity. In silence and in the exquisite light of a unique night, we walked back to our meeting room. I was certain that the wolf spirit experience was over. But I was wrong.

People quietly entered the room, lit in subtle golden hues of lamp light. Rather than returning to their place in our circle, however, several began to congregate at the far side of the space, lying down next to each other, bodies touching, as one would imagine wolves would do on a cold winter night. Some people, or should I say wolves, began to rub against one another, not in a sexual way as far as I could determine, but clearly expressing affection. I felt like the sorcerer's apprentice in Fantasia; what had our group and the spirit of wolf unleashed? In the interests of knowledge, I was curious to see what would transpire, fully setting limits within my mind as to what would be acceptable. Something important was happening.

I looked around, and to my disappointment, I noticed two women standing aside with very worried looks on their faces. I felt that I had to assuage what I construed to be their great fear, of what I cannot say; the unknown I suppose. In the role of workshop leader, one must be sensitive to all students. We were sailing in somewhat unchartered seas; this activity was a bit of an experiment. So, reluctantly, I beat on my drum again—four drum rolls, the signal to halt the activity. What I sensed next was palpable. The spirit of the wolf rose up into the air from the "pack" and began to drift northward out of the meeting room, into the night. I could sense the slow and steady movement of what seemed to be a great, powerful spirit away from the room, away from us.

Lessons were learned that night. First, if you call them, they will come. We called on the spirit of the wolf, and wolf spirits answered the call. Through merging with a specific species, we can experience being that species. It is said that you cannot know what it's like to be someone else until you have walked in their shoes. The group walked in the paws of the wolf. Most members of our group learned about the innocence of wildness, about the authenticity of the wild creatures that we call wolves. We learned that spirit wolves are willing to teach us and empower us—despite what humans have done to wolves—poisoning them, trapping them, shooting them, demonizing them. Some members of the group learned about the power of their own fears, which seemed to distort their perception of what had actually been transpiring. Personally, I learned that the spirits can surprise us, giving us positive and unforgettable experiences.

After some minutes of silence, we talked about our experiences with the spirit of wolf. Most, if not all, agreed that it had been a valuable, wonderful night. I have no doubt that 20 years later, many have a vivid recollection of that evening.

As I was clearing out some old papers and correspondence this year, I came upon a long forgotten letter sent to me two months after the workshop by one of the participants:

Hi. I recently attended one of your Basic Workshops on shamanism at the Keys Institute in Key Largo, FL. During that time someone requested we all 'experience' howling at the moon one night and the evening following this request, that's exactly what we did, calling on wolf medicine. It was an awful lot of fun and I'll never forget it. I'm writing at this time to share with you something very interesting that I just finished reading. One co-worker brought in a book on wolves and loaned it to me for the evening. When I got to page 22, I couldn't help but take special note of the information regarding ancient Roman wolf priests who celebrated something called the festival of Lupercalia—on February 15th. Of course, I immediately consulted the calendar regarding the night we were all engaged in our 'wolfness' and found it to have been Saturday night, February 15th. I believe this is what you would call a synchronicity. and thought you might get a kick out of it. I did!

Rome, of course, was founded by Romulus and Remus who had been suckled by the She-wolf. During Lupercalia, the Roman wolf priests, their naked bodies covered in the blood of a goat, would parade through the city "scourging any woman that they met with sanctified goat hair to ensure her fertility…The ritual invokes predation and death with blood of the goat, sexuality with naked dancing…participants receive the promise of fertility, new life."

3 | THE INCENSE BURNER

In the autumn of 1985, I received a short letter from Michael Harner in which he strongly recommended that I attend the late January 1986 Foundation for Shamanic Studies (FSS) Month-Long Training at Esalen Institute on the Big Sur coast of California. I was ecstatic to receive the note and to contemplate the prospect of studying shamanism with him at the world famous New Age center located in one of the most beautiful places on the planet.

Harner had gotten to know me in Rye, NY at the first East Coast Harner Method Shamanic Counseling Training in May, 1985. There, a small group of students, gathered at Wainwright House, were among the first to explore Harner's simultaneous narration technique, a powerful approach to the shamanic journey. It was a week of excitement and discovery and of making new friends. During one counseling journey, acting as the client, I experienced a profound fear which seemed to be the same fear that I had felt in a recurring childhood nightmare. It seemed important to tolerate that fear as long as possible during the journey; at a certain point, however, it became unbearable, and I returned back to ordinary consciousness and ordinary reality.

Since then, I have never again experienced the feeling of helplessness and foreboding evoked during that journey and those childhood dreams.

My job at *The Washington Post* allowed me a great deal of freedom, and I was able to secure five weeks off from work to attend the Month-Long Training. A friend had asked me to join her at her family's dairy farm in southeastern Wisconsin prior to my flying to California. I had wanted to visit a Wisconsin dairy farm since childhood, and for years I had dreamed of visiting Esalen Institute. It was time for dreams to come true.

I was treated warmly by my friend's parents, who owned and worked the farm. One special night, the family clan gathered for a euchre tournament. The snow lay silently outdoors, the cows were contentedly resting in their barn, and we all had enjoyed a satisfying potluck supper. Since I was unfamiliar with euchre, the card game was explained to me, the city slicker, as four tables were being set up for the 16 players. Games are played and when they conclude, players switch tables and partners, with individual scores being kept. Quickly, I began to be dealt some of the luckiest hands in the history of the game. By the end of the tournament on that memorable night, the novice from DC had smeared the competition. I won't forget how irritated my friend's brother-in-law was at my good fortune.

At the conclusion of my short visit, I was driven to Madison and flew in a snowstorm to Minneapolis to catch a non-stop DC-10 flight to San Francisco. After spending the night at my restaurateur cousin's apartment in the city, I boarded a bus the next day, Sunday, to travel to Monterey where a shuttle would meet me and other training participants and take us to Esalen. The green central California hills were a contrast to the white world of Wisconsin and the washed out wintry world of the DC area. At the bus station in Monterey, I met Doug, Bert and Bea, who would be my friends and compatriots for the next month. I heard Bert say that shamanism had saved his life. As the sun was setting, the shuttle took us 40 miles down the coast on US 1, the spectacular twisting two-lane road that rises high above the Pacific next to steep coastal cliffs. The adventure was shaping up!

Arriving at Esalen in the dark, we were led to our rooms at The Big House, the site of our training and the house where Esalen co-founder Michael Murphy once lived. We met with Michael Harner at 8pm and embarked on the last month-long intensive that the Foundation for Shamanic Studies would ever offer. Michael began each session of the training by lighting a candle and the special incense from Maine that he preferred. The odor of that incense is central to this story.

I have many memories from that time: learning important shamanic healing and divinatory techniques, speaking with my fellow students, walking the beautiful grounds and looking out at the vast Pacific, watching whales parade along the coast, breathing in the aromatic air full of the scents of eucalyptus and sage, bathing in the golden light of the temperate climate, not having to cook for 30 days, being dismayed by the unfriendliness of the permanent Esalen residents, lounging in the famous hot tubs clinging at the top of the hundred foot high cliffs, enjoying an evening visit by Stanislav Grof (father of Holotropic Breath Work), and so on. Esalen is a sacred spot; if you look at current reviews of the Esalen Institute and its programs, you will find a wide variety of opinions—from stellar to dismal. But the land is magical and awesome.

At the close of an evening session early in the training, Michael asked us to be especially aware that night, as something important could happen. I went to my little room with some anticipation, which quickly dissolved into sleep. When I awoke the following morning the sun had risen, but something very much out of the ordinary was happening. As I lay in bed on my back, I sensed a presence on top of me. I nearly panicked as it seemed to press down on me. Would it suffocate me? I remembered something I had read somewhere; was it in one of Carlos Castaneda's books? All I had to do was push what I construed to be some sort of entity upward and vigorously breathe out, and perhaps I could rid myself of this being. I did these things and felt the presence fade away. I was enveloped in a sense of pride and couldn't wait to tell Michael what had happened.

At the morning session that day, I related my experience to him. His response was highly amusing; "Congratulations, you just blew the opportunity of a lifetime to communicate with a spirit. But you can journey back to that moment in time, talk to the spirit, and see what it has to say to you." I experienced elation, deflation, and hopefulness all in a matter of seconds.

That night, I put on my headphones, turned on the cassette player (the 'ancient' audio technology of the mid-1980s), and journeyed back to the event in question. The spirit, whose form I could not discern, told me that there was a spirit of a person roaming the grounds of Esalen. I realized this was why I had felt fear when walking around at night. Further, I should speak to the roaming spirit and offer my help. I did speak to this roaming spirit and offered to help it move on. The spirit declined; it was not yet time for it to leave this Middle World. After this series of events, I no longer felt discomfort walking alone in the darkness of Esalen.

A week or so into this delicious month-long course of study, an attractive anthropologist in her mid-30s appeared. She was an associate of Michael Harner who had been living with the Jívaro, or Shuar, people in Amazonia—the same tribe that was the subject of Michael's book, *The Jívaro*. Michael had spent 14 months with this fiercely independent shamanic people, formerly headhunters. The young anthropologist had suddenly become quite ill, returned to the U.S., and then consulted a physician, who told her that she had contracted a rare and deadly form of cancer. Michael determined that our group would attempt to help her in her fight to survive. With him acting as the main shaman, we worked for three straight nights and experienced the beauty of working on behalf of someone who really required shamanic help. Michael said that she had been bewitched by someone, probably one of the Shuar, whom she had offended somehow. The sorcerer, Michael explained, was not exercising good judgment in using spiritual means to hurt someone. The suffering promoted in someone else would come back to the perpetrator three fold. A number of us (particularly the men in our group) wanted our patient to remain with us and join the training. Michael, for good reason I'm sure, did not invite her to remain with us.

During this training, Michael asked me if I would be interested in presenting workshops for the FSS. His offer took me by surprise, and I asked him if he had consulted his helping spirits about this. He said that he had not. I replied that I would be very happy to present workshops for him and his organization. This was one of those really special opportunities that would determine the course of my life for decades. I'm glad that I accepted his offer.

The days flew by and finally it was time to say goodbye to our teacher, my new found friends, Esalen and the great Pacific Ocean. The day the training ended, Michael drove me to the Monterey airport where I rented a big burgundy Oldsmobile. I drove back to Esalen to pick up fellow students Bert and Doug. That evening, the rains began and continued through the night. The next day, a small mud slide covered 40 feet of US 1 just north of us. Our departure was delayed for a few hours until highway crews cleared US 1 of mud. We departed, planning to drop Doug off in San Francisco and then Bert and I would continue driving 70 miles north to Santa Rosa to spend the night at my Uncle Danny's place at Oakmont Retirement Community.

Two hours later, we were speeding through the Santa Cruz Mountains. Doug was sound asleep in the back seat. Bert was driving. For no particular reason, I began to whistle a song that Michael had taught us and we had sung many times during the past month. In a few seconds I noticed, with great surprise, the distinct odor of the incense which Michael had burned every day for the past month. It was unmistakably the scent of the Maine incense. Without giving Bert any clue, I simply asked him if he was noticing anything. For all he knew, I was directing his attention to the scenery we were driving through or to an unusual sound the car was making. He took a couple of deep inhalations through his nose and exclaimed, "Son of a gun, I can smell it, too!" The 'apprentice' had unintentionally summoned the spirits—in this case, the spirit of the incense smoke to which we had become accustomed. The spirit of the smoke had manifested physically, and two people had detected its presence. Twenty-seven years later, my wife Shana and I had dinner with Bert in Doylestown, PA, and I asked him if he could recall the incident. Indeed he could, with great clarity. Curiously, his experience was that the odor was not of the Maine incense, but of sage. Nevertheless, here was an example of two people experiencing the same sort of physical manifestation of spirit. In F. Bruce Lamb's excellent book *The Wizard of the Upper Amazon*, there is an account of several men in an Amazonian tribe having the same spiritual experience under the influence of a hallucinogen as they sought to help one of their compatriots.

I have reflected on this incident of the incense fragrance many times. I have concluded that the helping spirits we had met and with whom we had worked during that month had engineered the event. The appearance of the fragrances—the Maine incense and sage—was a powerful confirmation of the reality of the spirits and the spirit world. This was a gift that would remain with us forever; should we ever begin to doubt the existence and the compassion of the helping spirits, we need only recall that moment in the car, speeding through the coastal mountain forests of central California. We were reminded of what it is that the shaman knows.

We arrived in San Francisco at dusk and dropped Doug off. The sparkling city by the sea seemed particularly noisy and dirty; thirty days in the pristine wilderness of Big Sur, punctuated by a couple of trips to lovely Carmel, will spoil you and make you forget the downside of human congestion. We continued our journey and finally arrived at my uncle's house entirely too late. My mother's brother had retired as a high school vice principal. When he was younger he had been a movie and television extra. He had been a hero of mine when I was a boy, and we had briefly lived near him and his family in southern California. Bert pointed out the interesting statue placed near the front door to his condominium; it reminded us of the mysterious Easter Island statues.

We went to bed knowing we would be able to catch just a little sleep before driving south to the San Francisco airport the following morning. After breakfast there was a little time for Danny to drive us around his beautiful retirement community lying near the base of Sugarloaf Ridge's Bald Mountain, which rises to a height of 2,700 feet. He took us to one of the two golf courses on the property, mostly to show us a particular great oak tree. Oak trees dot the Oakmont landscape, home to various bird species, including the conspicuous Nuttal's Woodpecker.

Our visit to Danny and his wife Mary and the wine country of Sonoma County's Valley of the Moon was painfully brief. As Bert and I drove for two hours down Highway 101 to San Francisco Airport, he said, "You know, don't you, that your uncle is a shaman? He's got a statue of a Polynesian god and he worships an oak tree!" Bert could not have been more complimentary of my favorite uncle.

When I place the incense holder down on the Celtic knot motif dish, I think of the magic 'smoke' we inhaled in the Santa Cruz Mountains and, when there is time, I think of many of the events and people I have just described. The memories speak of power, beauty, companionship, the presence of the helping spirits, and just plain fun.

4 | THE RING & THE DRUMBEATER

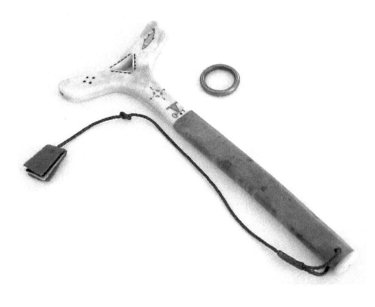

I first met Ailo Gaup in 1989 during the first week of the first East Coast Three-Year Program of the Foundation for Shamanic Studies taking place in Upstate New York. I'd heard stories of the man, good stories of this Sami shaman/novelist from Norway. I felt just a bit nervous when I was introduced to this engaging fellow of the Great North late Sunday night in the kitchen of the Phoenicia, NY Pathwork Center, tucked away in a quiet valley in the Catskills, where we would meet six times for six-day trainings. He quickly dispelled my anxiety with his warmth and genuine interest in me. Also, scrounging for late night snacks tends to promote camaraderie. We would get to know each other well in the ensuing two and a half years of the training.

The Sami are the native peoples of northern Scandinavia and have a long tradition of shamanism, although the invaders from the south, the Europeans, did their best to stamp out shamanism and replace it with their brand of Christianity: the *modus operandus* was believe what we believe, or you may be exterminated—P.S., no drums allowed. The Sami are the reindeer herders—people of the earth and the wind, the darkness, the sun, and the sea. The Norwegians, in particular, and the German Nazis, made a religion out of stamping out Sami culture. Sami children were sent to missionary schools, Sami human rights were limited, Sami lands ravaged. This has a familiar ring to those of us in the western world. One wonders when this sort of behavior on the part of those who worship money and temporal power will altogether cease. And if it doesn't, will our planet eventually be uninhabitable for our species, not to mention all other species? Thankfully, in at least some parts of Sápmi, or Sami Land, the authorities are treating this indigenous people in a more enlightened way.

When I think of Ailo, I see him wandering through the Catskill forest singing his personal soul songs, at least part of the time yoiking. The yoik (or joik) is "a form of song which utilizes a scale and vocalizations which are unfamiliar to virtually everyone in the Western (American and European) world; the history of the yoik is representative of all the encroachment and abuse that the Sami people have suffered at the hands of outsiders."[1]

In his singing walks, Ailo displayed a naturalness and childlike joy that I admired, even envied. He seemed to melt into the landscape of trees and rocks and ancient, rounded mountains. Simply by being, he was a teacher. And he continued to share his wisdom with those fortunate and wise enough to listen through his workshops and books.

---

1   http://www.utexas.edu/courses/sami/diehtu/giella/music/yoiksunna.htm, August, 2013.

On the fourth six-day installment of the FSS East Coast Three-Year Program, Ailo told me that he had something for me. My initial reaction, which I kept to myself, was, *Uh, oh, what is this about*? He handed me the object that lies at the center of my altar, a Sami style drumbeater made of birch wood and caribou antler.

He said, "This was made for me. Now I give it to you." I was humbled by his generosity and attentiveness to me. I examined the beater and noticed the scrimshawing on the semicircular antler portion of the beater. Ailo explained the meaning of the symbols. One symbol was easily recognizable: a shaman holding a drum. The triangular hole in the antler is a passageway to the spirit world. One simply holds the beater with that opening pressed against a closed eye and moves out into the spirit world, away from this physical world.

I showered Ailo with thanks and immediately began thinking of an appropriate gift to give to him when our next session would be held. Within a few minutes, I decided to present him with a very special beaded pouch given to me by its maker, a Cree Nation medicine woman, Rose Auger. (More about Rose in the following chapter.) Four months later, in October 1991, our group met once again. I hurried to find Ailo; I couldn't wait to give him the gift and see his reaction.

"Hey, Ailo! I have something for you," I said. He seemed quite interested. I handed him the pouch, made of soft leather and bright beading. He admired the object, then looked directly at me and said "Thanks."

He quickly followed with a surprising question. "Does it hurt you to give me this?"

I was taken aback but answered honestly. "Yes, it really does hurt." I was very fond of this gift from Rose and quite attached to it.

Then Ailo laughed his hearty Sami laugh, coming from somewhere deep within his being, and said, "You know, Dana, I was in pain for weeks after I gave you the drumbeater."

Perhaps the most interesting people are those who perpetually surprise. The temporary pain I experienced was soon replaced by the joy I felt in knowing that the gift pleased Ailo and that each time he looked at or touched the object, he would no doubt think of me.

Lying above the drumbeater on the altar is a brass ring with flattened sides that Ailo gave to all 60 or so participants in that Three-Year Program. He explained that the ring was a copy of one found in the eye socket of a polar bear skull unearthed in Norway's tundra. The Sami hunted reindeer, fish and marine mammals, moose, ptarmigan, as well as bears. "Bear hunting also played an important function in Sami culture and religion...although the bear was eaten, a ceremony was performed to appease its spirit. The bones were then placed in correct anatomical position and were buried in a grave."[2] Michael Harner surmised that the ring may have been placed in the bear skull's eye socket to serve as a tunnel assisting the bear's spirit to leave this world and travel to the next; it was certainly placed there as part of an honoring process. One wonders how modern

2   http://www.utexas.edu/courses/sami/diehtu/siida/hunting/jonsa.htm, August 2013.

humans can eat animals and thereby sustain their own lives without the slightest thought of paying homage to the slaughtered innocent beings whose sacrifice, whether voluntary or not, perpetuates the lives of the meat eaters.

After our final five-day session, Ailo presented a two-day workshop on Sami shamanism that some of us attended. Early in the workshop he encouraged us to find a place in the North, a special spirit place. What follows is my journey experience in that particular search.

I follow reindeer tracks northward, over northern landscapes. The snow gets deep as we traverse through blizzards. The tracks go past a cave in the side of a mountain. I see the reindeer run off. I'm drawn into the cave. There is a polar bear in there in front of a fire. I lie down next to the bear. We are friends. He sends me to the back of the cave where there is a door. I open the door and see many jewels. Beyond the jewels is a great heart pumping. Inside the heart is a vast nothingness. A polar bear appears; he is dancing. I begin to dance. I am dancing with the bear. I begin to transform into a polar bear. Dancing together, we pop out of the mountain and begin roaming the landscape. We are huge. I mark the territory of the bear, the Great North. This is his territory. Then I am called back by the change in the drumbeat. And I change back into human form.

I had not read this account for many years. Upon rereading it, I was deeply moved, and my relationship with the polar bear invigorated. It begs a question: how many significant journeys (at least in the mind of the journeyer) must one experience in order for some sort of transformation to occur? That transformation might entail a significant realization of one's true place on our planet, or perhaps one simply becomes a kinder person; possibly one realizes that human consciousness is just one more consciousness on the planet, not superior to any of the other millions of consciousnesses we share this awesome blue orb with. Could just one journey make a difference? Harner relates how Indian yogis he worked with felt that they had made more progress in a single journey than they had in years of yogic meditative practice.

In speaking of singing, so important for the Sami, Ailo told us that our pain can prevent us from singing. Behind the pain, there is a bird waiting to sing; harmony waits to be expressed. These are songs of the spirit. The bird lives in our throat; the hunters, human and animal, live in our abdomens.

Again I went to the polar bear who took me into the sea and to an underwater town where many polar bears lived. They danced for me, I danced for them. Then the bear who was my companion and I sat and looked out at the sea world. He told me that compassion was a critical component of my psyche and that I needed as much of it as I could incorporate into my being.

In another journey, Ailo asked us to travel to the sun and then follow a fiber of light to meet a shaman related to us. He said that we all come from enlightened persons. It is valuable to meet such a person, who is an ancestor, and learn what gift that person has given us:

I followed a web line out to another time to a skin clothed shaman who was happy to see me. I asked what I needed to know. He said that I should practice exercising restraint because I have strong impulses. I should just observe those impulses. I need not act on them. I asked him what he has meant to me all of this time. He said that he has been watching over me and he has given me my wildness.

Ailo told me that this is my tradition, that this being that I met is backing me and is working on my behalf. The things I learned working with Ailo for two days are as helpful now as they were 21 years ago.

The gifts from Ailo—the drumbeater and ring—rest on my altar to remind me that Europe was once home to many shamans and my ancestors; thanks to the FSS and teachers such as Ailo, shamanism has returned to the British Isles and the Continent. The items are a tribute to my friendship with Ailo and symbolize three years of shamanic training presented by Michael Harner and the FSS and the power in which we were immersed during that time.

5 | THE POST CARDS, BEANIE
BABIES, ROCKS & THINGS

Some of the post cards and beanie babies on the altar depict animal spirit helpers; some of the creatures represented are simply favorite animals of mine. In the upper left hand corner are two pictures of manatees, the top one a photo of a painting. Manatees are large aquatic mammals living in the waters of the West Indies, the Amazon River, West Africa and Florida. They can grow to be thirteen feet in length and can weigh up to 3,500 pounds. They and the dugongs belong to the order of *Sirenia*.

In the winter of the year 2000, after teaching a workshop in the Tampa area, I drove to the town of Crystal River, 70 miles north, and spent the night at the Plantation Golf Resort and Spa. Early the following morning, the temperature having dipped into the low 40's, I walked over to the nearby dive shop. I had made an appointment to be taken out into the river equipped with a rented wet suit, face mask and flippers to swim with manatees. The water in the spring fed Crystal River is a constant 72 degrees, warm enough for manatees needing refuge from colder Gulf of Mexico winter temperatures.

We arrived at what was deemed to be a suitable spot. I slid into the water, which seemed particularly cold, probably due to the cold air, and started looking for manatees. I spotted one in the distance in the crystal clear river, gnawing on an anchor rope. Pursuing a manatee is illegal in Florida. I knew that I had to simply wait and see if any manatees would approach me. The minutes passed and my body began to chill. As I was just about to give up in my efforts to get close to one of these creatures, one appeared seemingly out of nowhere and approached me. This was a large adult. It positioned itself next to me, I reached out to touch the manatee, and then it began to revolve like a cement mixer, my hand still touching its elephant-like skin. Soon, another manatee joined us. I was outnumbered and nearly surrounded by two very large beings. Suddenly, as mysteriously as they had appeared, they were gone.

I swam back to the boat, which then took me back to the dive shop. I was in a hot shower very soon afterwards. I felt great satisfaction at having accomplished my goal of having an encounter with one of these amazing beings. The ease with which they move through the water is striking. One could never guess that they can move in bursts up to 20 mph. But even more amazing to me was the gentleness of this species. If only the human race could be so gentle, not to mention non-acquisitive and non-territorial. According to the Save the Manatee Club, of which I have been a member for fifteen years, many manatee deaths are human-related. Up to ninety percent of adult manatees have been scarred by motor boat propellers, according to biologist Kathryn Curtin.

I revisited the manatees in 2008 with my wife Shana, this time at the Homosassa River, near the spot of my first encounter. On the way down the river to a shallow cove overseen by Florida state authorities, we observed two dolphins herding a school of fish against a river sea wall, concentrating them to make feeding easier. Shana was as impressed as I was with the gentle manatees we found upon reaching the cove. At one point, a young manatee approached us to be touched. Despite being vulnerable to the deadly effects of cold, red tide, as well as human incursion, the manatees demonstrate to us how to live in harmony with nature rather than at odds with the natural world. When I see their pictures on the altar, I am reminded of the lessons they have to teach and of the love and respect that I feel for all wild creatures.

The shaman is closely in touch with that wildness. He works intimately with specific animal spirits of great power that we call Power Animals. The shaman, on occasion, will ask those beings to merge with him, in order to honor them and to keep their power, which is like protection, nearby. In merging with these spirits, the shaman embodies their wildness, which in my experience, is nurturing. In connecting with the primeval, one rests in the cradle of the universe. Life developed here on earth because of the chance confluence of a number of conditions. Lately, I have been thinking that life developed because it is simply the nature of matter to organize as life. This was the grand design of the Big Bang. Life has played out in millions of ways on Earth. The consciousness of each species is unique and valuable.

Species come and go, adding an element of particular poignancy to the existence of every species. Even the magnificent dinosaurs, with the exception of their bird descendants, disappeared. The human race must ultimately become sensitized to the needs of all creatures because the refusal to live in harmony with them and our environment can logically end only in our own disappearance. Extinction may simply be a given, since conditions are perpetually changing in the physical world. If we are hastening our own demise, and we seem to be, why must we take thousands of other species with us into oblivion?

Below the manatee images on the altar lies a card depicting a horse and the earth given to me by Dr. Geo Athena Trevarthen, a practitioner, author and teacher of Celtic Shamanism now living in Scotland. For me, the card evokes the multidimensionality of the physical universe. It is a reminder for me of Geo's gifts to the world and of her limitless faith in the spirits. The card also calls to mind the concept of an infinite number of probable worlds as described by Jane Roberts as she channeled the entity known as Seth. In books like *The Nature of Personal Reality* and *Seth Speaks*, Jane/Seth sets forth a fantastic description of the universe that is both plausible and hopeful: our reality is determined by our beliefs. We can change that reality if we change our beliefs. I had discounted the value of channeled books until I finally read Jane Roberts. Afterwards, I had a deep appreciation for the wisdom residing 'out there.'

Speaking of the shamanism of the northern European tribal peoples known as the Celts, Tom Cowan, writer and teacher and an authority on the subject, writes in his book *Fire in the Head,* "That rich strain of mysticism, which the Romans labeled superstition, was in fact the backbone of Celtic spirituality. It is also the philosophical basis for shamanism, a feature that makes the Celt, ancient or modern, a prime candidate for shamanic experiences...there was probably never a time, nor will there ever be, when the true Celt does not believe in the unseen Otherworld and the possibility of journeying there to discover the mysteries of the divine universe." My ancestry is Celtic, and though I have not identified with it as much as others have, it courses through my blood and cannot be ignored.

The photo in the bottom left corner of the altar was taken in the Everglades at sunset by my friend F.K. Jones, a former Fish and Wildlife Director for the Miccosukee Tribe of southern Florida. The last time I spoke with F.K. he was tracking the Florida panther in the 'Glades for the tribe. This magnificent species, whose existence is severely endangered, is a subspecies of the cougar. Thankfully, its numbers have increased in the last 40 years in Florida. The perpetuation of this species is dependent on a number of factors, including the health of the Everglades themselves. The amazing River of

Grass, declared a National Park in 1947, is a collection of various ecosystems, including freshwater sloughs, marl prairies, forests, wet prairies, salt marshes, and bodies of water up to 800 square miles in size. Unfortunately, the Everglades have suffered mightily from human incursions such as canals, drainage, forest harvesting, and the introduction of non-indigenous species, most notably of late the Burmese python. *National Geographic Magazine* has given the Everglades National Park and nearby Big Cypress National Preserve the lowest score of the dozens of national parks it recently reviewed in terms of quality, management and sustainable tourism.

I have often said that the entire Florida peninsula should have been declared a national park 170 years ago. It was a fabulous place teeming with life. The Native Americans would have been the only humans allowed to permanently live there. Development as we know it would have been forbidden. Instead, we have an example of human behavior at its worst: rampant greed, callousness, racism, sheer stupidity, short-sightedness, environmental irresponsibility. When a thoughtful person, respectful of beauty and all life forms, considers what has happened to the Everglades and even "Old Florida," he realizes that the divide between him and the despoilers and the uncaring is enormous.

My favorite author is John D. MacDonald, the author of the 21-book Travis McGee mystery series as well as more than 50 other books, mostly crime fiction; Stephen King calls MacDonald "the great entertainer of our age and a mesmerizing storyteller." Kurt Vonnegut has written, "To diggers a thousand years from now, the works of John D. MacDonald would be a treasure on the order of the tomb of Tutankhamen." Many of John D's novels (I have all of them) are set in Florida, including his well-known *Condominium* as well as the excellent *A Flash of Green*. Raised in upstate New York, he ultimately settled in Sarasota, one of America's most beautiful towns, and home to wide quartz-white powdered sand beaches and teeming-with-life Sarasota Bay. His works and his hero McGee often decry the despoliation of America's only tropical state. Amazingly, Random House has just announced that it will be publishing all 70 of MacDonald's books. Many have been out-of-print for some time.

McGee/MacDonald is a keen observer of humanity and its penchant for destruction. Witness this passage from *A Deadly Shade of Gold* (Gold Medal, 1965):

This is the virus theory of mankind. The pretentious virus, never knowing that it is a disease. Imagine the great ship from a far galaxy which inspects a thousand green planets and then comes to ours and, from on high, looks down at all the scabs, the buzzings, the electronic jabberings, the poisoned air and water, the fetid night glow. A little cave-dwelling virus mutated, slew the things which balanced the ecology, and turned the fair planet sick. An overnight disease, racing and explosive compared with geological time. I think they would be concerned. They would be glad to have caught it in time. By the time of their next inspection, a hundred thousand years hence, this scabrous growth might have infected this whole region of an unimportant galaxy. They would push the button. Too bad. This happens every once in a while. Make a note to re-seed it the next time around, after it has cooled down.

The works of John D display the insights of a non-ordinary reality Teacher, a spirit of great wisdom in human form that we work with in divination and healing. I highly recommend all of his works, from *A Friendship: the Letters of Dan Rowan and John D. MacDonald* to *The Damned*, a short novel of the good, the bad and the ugly waiting to board a river ferryboat; from *Please Write for Details,* a fictional piece about a writers' workshop in Mexico, to *Nothing Can Go Wrong,* the story of John D and his wife's 70+ day luxury liner cruise to Europe and back. Recently, I gave a friend a couple of MacDonald books. He told me that his life will never be the same as he feels compelled to read all of them now.

I've traveled to Florida nearly 80 times: including the Keys, Miami, Jacksonville, Boca, Orlando, Tallahassee, Tampa, Naples, and beyond. When we're driving along the Sunshine Skyway from Tampa's airport south to Sarasota, our hearts become full at the sight of Tampa Bay's sparkling waters and the pelicans, ospreys, egrets, ibises, and the other wonderful birds of Florida, 'the flowery land.' The cloud people are ever present, quietly attracting our attention. Despite the ravages of human incursion, Florida retains an aura of the magical. The simple photo of an Everglades sunset honors the creatures, the land, the workshop participants, the friends, a great writer, and the beauty and power of that part of our planet.

On top of the bear card, lying next to the bear Beanie Baby is a piece of bear fur. A singularly interesting Sioux, let's call him Jay, tore the fur from a much larger piece that served as his medicine bundle and gave it to me. He told me that the bundle had been given to him by his grandfather, a medicine man of the Sioux Nation. Jay was a Navy Seal medic in the Vietnam War and is a rehabilitator of problem horses. He is a chemist who was called upon to help a baby elephant at the Washington National Zoo that had become quite ill. Obviously, he has inherited the healing gifts of his grandfather.

A medicine bundle is a container of some sort, such as a pouch or piece of tied up animal skin, holding a collection of items with spiritual significance for the owner. For instance, a pouch might contain items that are reminders of powerful spiritual events in the owner's life. Norman Hunt, in his book _Shamanism in North America,_ states,

> _Among the Mide priests of the Great Lakes tribes, ritual paraphernalia were kept in a medicine bag when not in use. Different degrees of shamanic power were reflected in the animal skin used for the bag...and power was transferred to an initiate during the ritual by pointing or touching the initiate with the medicine bag._

In the compilation entitled *Stones, Bones and Skin*, Alika Webber writes, "a shaman's bag...contained the entire universe of the shaman who could bring it under his dominance." Thomas Mails, in his book *Plains Indians,* tells us of the importance of the bear knife bundle and the Beaver medicine bundle among the Blackfoot people. "Bear power for healing and war was transferred with the knife bundle...The duties of the owner of the Beaver bundle did not end with either the ceremonial planting or the harvesting, for he was believed, like beavers, to have the power to forecast the weather."

Jay is a warrior/healer. It seems very appropriate that his medicine bundle, a piece of which rests in my care, is comprised of bear fur, healing being associated with the bear. Mails states, "The bear was a great healing agent, and Bear (cult) members (of the Blackfeet) usually possessed healing abilities." Jay shared some special wisdom with me once. He said that modern people involved with shamanism too often look for the big experience, and by doing so, miss the subtle experience; and in that subtle experience was something that actually embodied great power and meaning, but it was ignored or overlooked because the focus was on the spectacular. People look for the hurricane and miss the gentle puff of wind that passes by their ear that really contains the answer or insight that they were looking for. In short, in doing shamanism, one should maintain a broad level of awareness.

As I look at the bear fur, I recall a significant event in my life. I was camping in the Shenandoah National Park in the summer years ago. One day, I went on a ten mile circuit hike, down a mountain and then back up. The day was warm. Midway in the trek, I came to a stream which had pooled nicely to a depth of four feet. I took off my clothes and immersed myself in the cold, clear water. After drying off and dressing, I continued my walk. After a few minutes, on my right in a small clearing, I spotted a bear seated upon a tree stump, grooming himself. He was no more than a hundred feet away. I was surprised and unprepared for an encounter with a bear, but quickly began to strategize. Should I stop and observe the bear or continue walking? Should I be as quiet as possible or purposely make some noise? Just as I determined that I would keep moving, the bear glanced at me, our eyes met, and he charged away up a nearby hill at the speed of a bolting horse.

Something happened to me in that moment when the bear's eyes met mine before he fled. I felt that I was in the presence of profound innocence. I understood that I, an adult human, was not innocent. More than anything, my lack of innocence was related to my own self-consciousness, my own mind and my own typically human behavior. I glimpsed the chasm between humans and the rest of the living world and understood the meaning of the fall from Grace, the expulsion from the Garden. I felt a sense of loss that I wish that every human would feel, because that could obliterate the human sense of superiority which leads to such disastrous results. I felt a compassion for all of the wild creatures of this impossibly wondrous planet. I was humbled by the beautiful bear, the one who still lives in The Garden. In the next life, I hope that I will live in the Peaceable Kingdom with my bear brothers and sisters.

As we know, the slaughter of the innocent ones continues without interruption. In my fantasies, I dream of commanding aircraft carriers that follow Japanese and Icelandic whaling ships and order the killers to immediately cease the slaughter or else! I think that if you kill a dolphin, you should be arrested for murder. I know that you need not take LSD or drink ayahuasca or dime or chew peyote buttons to understand that every ant, every eagle, every tree, every fox, every shark is our brother or sister and that fratricide is an abomination. It is clear that it is the duty of humans, as they make decisions, to consider all living beings on the planet. Every living thing, including the rocks, the rivers, the soil and the air (as the Chukchee say, everything that *is* is alive) has fifteen billion years of evolution behind it. Who are we to destroy anything? If we don't change our ways, it will be recorded that we were the Great Destroyers, the clever ones who, in truth, were stupid and cruel beyond imagination. There's a saying out on the streets: "what goes around, comes around." We have been warned. Joni Mitchell was correct in singing at Woodstock, "We've got to get ourselves back to The Garden." As a Baby Boomer I wonder what became of my generation which started so promisingly and spoke of Cultural Revolution, only to fall farther than our parents did into the abyss of materialism.

Just below the drum beater on my altar is a U.S. Army Ranger patch. It was given to me years ago by a young man in his late 20s. He told me that he had been in the Rangers and had loved it, but it had dawned on him that working with troubled youth would bring him even greater joy and satisfaction. And so he resigned from the Rangers and followed the path with greater heart. I told him that I thought that had been a very fine thing to do. The following day he presented me with a Ranger patch. It reminds me of the importance of being true to oneself, of giving up something which seems good for something even better. It is emblematic of discipline, for the Rangers certainly embody that quality. The proper practice of shamanism involves a high level of discipline: when one journeys out, one always returns; we believe that we work for others only when others request the work; we stay focused on our shamanic mission but are also open to unexpected gifts from the spirits; we never use spiritual means to hurt anyone; even in an activity as simple as drumming, we concentrate on keeping a steady drumbeat.

The patch is also a reminder of my past, for I am the son of a U.S. Army career officer. My father was a brilliant man who achieved the rank of Lieutenant Colonel without attending a single day of college. On the walls of our homes were displayed numerous commendations and expressions of thanks from those for whom he worked. He once told me that he had read the philosopher Schopenhauer when he was 13 years old. I will make a small leap in saying that Schopenhauer's thought, influenced by Eastern religion, was in part shamanic. His view of animals was that they were essentially our equals. He emphasized the importance of compassion. My father, who grew up amongst the potato fields of eastern Long Island, embodied many of this philosopher's thoughts, and I have come to realize that I am my father's son.

A short story: we moved from a Tidewater Virginia army base in 1959 to the Azores, lovely islands in the mid-Atlantic ocean, and left behind our beloved tri-color collie, Ring, with friends. News reached us that Ring was very unhappy, and we missed him terribly. Additionally, somehow Ring had acquired a severe wound to his head. My father decided to bring Ring to the Azores and caught various military transport propeller planes, not speedy jets, to Tidewater and then returned a few days later to our island home with our dog. These are the actions of a man with deep compassion.

He worked with USAID in Vietnam in the late 1960's after retiring from the Army. When my draft number came up low in 1972 when I was 26 years old, my father, truly a man of peace, told me that I must not go to Vietnam as a soldier. I obeyed. The Ranger patch serves as a remembrance of my youth as an Army dependent, of the many tentative hellos and bittersweet goodbyes that I experienced as a nomad during the Golden Age of America in the late 1940's, the 1950's and the early 1960's, and of my father who now dwells in the Upper World with my mother.

The polished stones below the bear card and Beanie Baby were given to me by Jeff, a fine student of shamanism. The changes over the years that I have observed in this man have been significant. I have seen him adopt a stance of far greater humility, and I attribute this to not only the continuing natural maturation process but also to his working with the great, compassionate spirits that we meet in shamanism. Michael Harner has said that in doing shamanism, we become better people. I believe that we are influenced by those with whom we associate. If I associate with politicians, I am more likely to be superficial and corrupt. If I work intimately with great spirit allies that I have met in the Upper or Lower World, I am more likely to be an ethical, sensitive, compassionate person. When I see these polished rocks on my altar, I think of the power of shamanism to promote positive change; and I think of the "rock people," the oldest inhabitants of our planet, who stoically stand by as events whirl around them.

To the left of the drumbeater is a small leather "prayer tie." Prayer ties, typically small red, white, yellow or black cloth pouches containing tobacco or herbs, are found in Native American sweat lodges strung from the lodge framework. They are constructed while prayers are enunciated. This particular prayer tie was given to me by a Cherokee man who said that he was learning shamanism so that he could return to his people in North Carolina and teach them the shamanic journey and some of the other simple, but profound techniques of the shaman.

I have included the feathers of macaws, turkeys and blue jays on the altar. Birds are one of my great joys—the masters of two worlds (land and air), sometimes three (land, water, and air). People devote their lives to studying, observing and/or helping these wondrous beings. I try to notice them each day. Blue jays come to my backyard each morning for their peanuts in shells—I gladly oblige them. The sugar water feeders in front of our house are visited frequently by speedy and darting hummingbirds during spring and summer. Driving on the back roads of the Delmarva Peninsula where we live, we have seen as many as a dozen eagles dancing in the wind with their brothers and sisters, the vultures.

After reading Dr. Robert Bakker's amazing book, *The Dinosaur Heresies*, I understand that the great dinosaurs are still with us in the form of earth's birds. Of course, the non-feathered beings—some immense, some small, that we normally think of being dinosaurs—are gone. Dr. Bakker does not attribute their extinction to the great meteorite hit 65 million years ago, the so-called Cretaceous-Paleocene Extinction Event, but to the shifting of land masses which severely upset the balance of nature. Very little imagination is required to recognize that if the largest and most powerful of all animals, who roamed the earth for tens of millions of years, can become extinct, so then can the human race. I honor the birds for their beauty and intelligence, and as descendants of the dinosaurs, for reminding us of the fragility of existence and the absurdity of taking very much of anything for granted.

The object to the right of the wallet is a buffalo tooth; to the left of the wallet is a silver buffalo head pin; and central is the beaded wallet depicting the buffalo. The buffalo is a symbol for me of quiet, immense strength and the power of innocence. Once there were 50 million of these incredible creatures roaming the plains; now there are perhaps 200,000. It's difficult to conceive of the senseless slaughter of these magnificent beings. What sort of species would murder so many innocent beings, no matter what the reason? The buffalo asks us to consider our own true nature. Are we simply the killer ape, with the peaceful among us being aberrations? Or is the opposite true? The slaughter of the innocents persists. What is our responsibility to animals and plants? Do they have the right to live out their lives as nature intended or are we, as humans, self-appointed determiners of the fate, not only of all beings, but of the Planet Earth itself? Are we a virus—an unfortunate evolutionary product, ultimately destroying everything that we can, as Travis McGee/John D. MacDonald suggests—or can we live in an enlightened way in harmony with all that is? I suggest that you look around and see for yourself what humanity has wrought; that you honestly appraise your role in the present condition of the planet and think about how you can be the most positive sort of force in the face of global desecration and destruction.

6 | THE BUFFALO WALLET

In 1982, a First Nations medicine woman, Rose Auger, "Woman Who Stands Strong," from northern Alberta, Canada gave a talk at the Bethesda, Maryland Food Co-Op. Her message was the importance of living in harmony with our Earth, with all of the inhabitants of our incredible planet. She embodied authority, sensitivity and intelligence. You knew that she walked her talk. I spoke with her after her presentation. Later in the week, I attended a two-day training of hers that she presented to a small group of people. In Bethesda, she talked about the work she was doing on behalf of her tribe, the Cree Nation; some of it involved helping people with addictions. She related the story of the potlatch, the great giveaway event of Native peoples, particularly of the Pacific Northwest. Once, she said, she gave away a pickup truck to someone, knowing that her own needs would always be taken care of. She was an impressive woman.

I obtained her address and began to send her some money in monthly installments as a token of my respect for her and her work. In the meantime, having attended the Basic Workshop of the Foundation for Shamanic Studies and an advanced Foundation training at

Grottoes, VA, I regularly met with spirit friends in the Upper World and connected with my personal spirit allies. One morning in February 1983, upon awakening and getting out of bed, I was overwhelmed by vertigo. The bedroom was spinning. I thought I was dying! So began an ordeal, both physical and emotional, that lasted five months. I was overcome by physical weakness. As long distance swimming and running were my main coping strategies, those days were difficult since I was unable to either run or swim. Medical doctors guessed that I had had an inner ear infection.

I had vivid dreams during that time. In one, I traveled downward in a spiral cave toward the voice of a child saying, "Help me, please help me." Was this some fragment of my soul calling out for help? My condition did improve through rest, but relapses occurred. Finally, after several months of trying to regain my strength, I wrote to Rose Auger, telling her of my condition. A week or so later, on a Saturday morning, I received a letter from her. In it, she stated, "I will speak to the 'Invisible Worlds' for you and you may feel a presence or even hear wings if they agree. Be happy!" The next morning, Sunday, I took a walk in my Takoma Park, MD neighborhood and passed a small flock of sparrows feeding in the front yard of a house. Although I was moving slowly and trying not to disturb the birds, they flew away as I walked by. I heard their wing beats!

Later that day, walking in Jequie Park, I heard the wing beats of crows in the tops of tall trees. This bordered on the impossible, as the park is next to the subway and railroad tracks and very close to noisy Piney Branch Road. I took note of having heard wings, but I had no expectations of anything coming out of these experiences. Nevertheless, I was keenly aware of what Rose had written, and I was certainly open to something wonderful happening. The next morning, after awakening, I had a surprising sense of well-being. After dressing, I felt with certainty that my condition of weakness and dizziness had been healed—completely. I was right! It turned out that Rose's efforts did result in my return to health and strength.

In August 1983, Rose returned to the Washington DC area. I organized a lecture for her at the old Takoma Café, a last vestige of the counter culture days of that town that I called home for 30+ years. The café was jammed with interested people. Speaking with her before her presentation, I asked her what in retrospect seems a silly question: "How many spirit helpers do you have?" She answered she had over four hundred. No wonder the healing was so successful! Later I learned that 405 is the traditional number of helping spirits that a Lakota is born with. The Cree are not Lakota, but one might assume cultural similarities between the two groups since they historically lived near each other, although not always peacefully. I presented another question to Rose: "Why did I become sick?" She said, "You became sick because you were not spiritual enough!" I had not told Rose about my studying with Michael Harner and taking many shamanic journeys, which would certainly qualify as spiritual work. The fact is, prior to the onset of my condition, I had ceased journeying and calling my spirit helpers (and their power) to me. Rose's explanation mirrored what had become of my spiritual life. I had learned some of the basics of shamanism and had applied them in my life. For some reason, perhaps laziness, I had dropped these practices and eventually, I had gotten sick.

At Rose's behest, her spiritual helpers had healed me. They had a choice—fortunately, they smiled upon me; as the saying goes, they took pity on me. I learned first-hand that spiritual healing was real. That is, through the use of spiritual methods, in this case the supplication of helping spirits, miraculous healing can result. I presented Rose with a special gift as a token of my great thanks for the help that she and her allies gave me. She told me of a man who had traveled to her home in Faust, Alberta, to receive healing. Ultimately he was healed. He thanked Rose and said that he would return to his home. Rose said that he should not return for it was his life back home that had made him sick.

My experience with Rose convinced me to renew my studies in shamanism. I chose to reconnect with Michael Harner. I felt a good deal of rapport with him, and he was a superb teacher. His sense of humor made learning a pleasure. In addition, most of his teaching then was conveniently occurring on the East Coast. Within three years, I was attending the month-long Foundation training at Esalen Institute.

One of Rose's students, Tom, conducted sweat lodges from time to time. He had learned 'water pouring' from Rose at her place in the North Country. I had great confidence in Tom because of that. One Saturday afternoon, my friend Russell and I drove out to Annapolis, MD to a private home located on several acres next to a wide tidal creek. Tom was holding a sweat lodge. Russell was unfamiliar with the process, but was and is a man with a great sense of adventure. Nearly 30 years later, Russell would be able to tell you in detail what he experienced that day. Suffice to say that the spirits manifested in dramatic ways in that lodge. (If I could sum up Michael Harner's latest book, *Cave and Cosmos*, in a sentence it would be this: The spirits are real. Based on the events in that lodge, the same conclusion holds. The spirits are real.)

Inside a sweat lodge, the darkness is punctuated only by glowing rocks brought in from a fire outside and placed in a hole in the center of the lodge. Amidst the steam heat created by the pouring of water onto the rocks, prayers are said by those in the lodge. At one point during the sweat lodge that evening in Annapolis, I felt the wings of a large bird batting against my head. I felt the softness of the feathers, the strength of the wings. I assure you that no one had brought bird wings into the lodge.

I think of Rose when I lay out my altar. She sent me the beaded wallet featuring the head of a buffalo, which has a central place on the altar. Rose did the beading on the wallet and on the pouch that she sent me. This was the pouch that I gave to Ailo Gaup, the present that I admitted pained me to give to him. Rose passed on to the next world in 2011. The loss for her people, for all people, is tremendous. I wonder if anyone can ever replace this treasure of a woman, this incredible healer. Some would say that regret is a frivolous, absurd emotion. But I have a regret concerning Rose; it's that I did not continue communicating with her, that I never trekked up to northern Alberta to say hello to her and perhaps learn from her, that I did not continue my friendship with her. Such regrets hopefully prevent us from having to experience similar regrets in the future. We are inclined to think that some opportunities will always be available to us; as time passes, we learn the uniqueness of the moment and learn that assumptions are often wrong.

7 | THE RATTLE, THE TOLI & THE TUVAN LAKE

Rattles can be used in lieu of drums to promote an altered state of consciousness. Monotonous percussion promotes the theta state of brain wave activity. Theta brain waves are associated with trance states and, not surprisingly, are found frequently in young children—childhood, the naturally visionary phase of life. When I build my altar, I don't normally place my rattle upon it; but later, during a workshop, I will place the rattle on the altar, a generally safe spot where the rattle can't be stepped on. Despite such precautions, at the conclusion of workshop I presented in Plantation, FL, the 10-year old daughter of my organizer accidentally stepped on my beloved gourd rattle that I had purchased at the Indian Craft Shop at the U.S. Department of the Interior and cracked it, rendering it useless.

Not long afterwards, I traveled to Santa Fe, NM to visit a friend. At the same time, the famous Santa Fe Indian Market was being held. In those days, the late 90s, the Market featured the works of six or seven hundred Native American artists and artisans. The sculptures, paintings, jewelry and other works on display evidenced great skill and artistry. Now a thousand artists have booths in downtown Santa Fe during Indian Market and more than 150,000 people from all over the world attend this remarkable event held in August of each year. I needed to replace my broken rattle and was surprised to find only a couple of artists selling them. One of them was Ralph Aragon, who lives at Zia Pueblo, 17 miles outside Albuquerque. I was impressed by the rattle he had made, and I told him that I would be happy to purchase the rattle and promote his work at my workshops. Ralph specializes in what he calls petroglyph art. His rattles, pots, shields and canvasses are inspired by the ancient art found on the rocks of the American Southwest.

A couple of years later, I visited New Mexico again to spend some time with my friend Russell (mentioned in the previous chapter) and his wife Kathy, who had moved there from Maryland. New Mexico is called "The Land of Enchantment," and a visit there will prove the truth of that description. The mountains and mesas, the vast sky, the colors, the rainbows, and the plants and animals in themselves promote an altered state of consciousness. I have rich memories of my time there. Russell accompanied me on my way back to Albuquerque. A professional pilot, he was on his way to the airport and was interested in joining me for a visit at Ralph's house at Zia. I had called Ralph and told him that I wanted to see him.

While my memory is vague, I recall the beauty of the place and the gracefulness of the dwellings. The vitality and timeless quality of the pueblo belied its six hundred year age. In fact, many Hollywood movies have been filmed at Zia because of its special qualities. Upon our arrival, Ralph, his wife Joan, and daughter Leslie welcomed us with great warmth. The two hours that we spent there are a very special memory. I speak with Ralph occasionally when I am ordering another rattle from him. The fact that he recognizes my voice and remembers me is something that makes me very happy. The rattles that I receive are incredible works of art as well as wonderful shamanic tools.

My Ralph Aragon rattle reminds me that what may be perceived as a loss can also be seen as an opportunity. My first rattle was squashed by the innocent young lady. This led to my acquiring other rattles of even greater beauty and functionality and to getting to know a very kind and very talented Native American artist.

Sometimes the toli, also called the shaman's mirror, finds its way onto my altar. The toli, a metal disc often made of brass, is a traditional tool of the Mongolian shamans, and the right to wear a toli comes through the Shanar or dedication ceremony. Virlana Tkacz, in her book *Shanar*, states that there are different Shanars for different tools used by the shamans of central and east Siberia including the drum, the drum stick, the headdress, the whip, the bell, the orgay or shaman's horns, the cape, and the staff. According to Sarangerel Odigan in her book, *Chosen by the Spirits*, "Shamans try to collect as many mirrors (tolis) as they can because they have tremendous protective and energizing power....The absorbing and radiating capabilities of a mirror come in handy for removal of intrusions and soul retrieval." Many tolis are very old—sometimes thousands of years old—and are passed down from one shaman to another.

The toli that I place on the altar was given to us by its maker, our good friend Heidi, who lives in central Florida. She has strong Buryat blood coursing through her body and her spirituality, for her grandfather was a Buryat shaman. Buryatia is an area around Lake Baikal in eastern Siberia. Home to 300,000 Buryats, it is renowned for its shamans. Heidi is in a direct line of Buryat shamans. She embodies the qualities one associates with an authentic shaman: power, quiet confidence, humility, a sense of humor, concern for all life on the planet. She is dedicated to the great helping spirits, to helping others, and is at once both teacher and student. The toli is a reminder of Heidi and of the shamans, present and past, who live in the heartland of shamanism—Siberia. In addition, it is a tool to be used. I wear it when singing a healing song to the sun.

Not far from Lake Baikal in eastern Siberia is the country of Tuva, formerly a Soviet Republic, and a land with a rich tradition of shamanism. The communists outlawed shamanism in Tuva, driving the practice underground. Since the breakup of the Soviet Union, shamanism has made a great comeback there due, in part, to the 1993 Foundation for Shamanic Studies expedition to Tuva. That 10-day field trip culminated with the President of Tuva speaking with members of the Foundation team. Afterwards he declared publicly that shamanism and Buddhism would be equally respected in the modern Tuvan Republic. Paul Uccusic, who was part of the original expedition, traveled on additional Foundation trips back to Tuva and was the head of the European branch of the Foundation for Shamanic Studies for many years. He was instrumental in bringing Tuvan shamanism to the Western World.

The post card on the lower right side of the altar depicts a Tuvan lake and was given to me by a woman who was a member of the Tuvan team that came to Sonoma, CA in 1996 to spend time with Foundation students. The card sparks my memory of a wonderful five days of sharing and learning. One of the Tuvans, shaman Ai-Churek Oiun, was very impressive in her sweet demeanor and absolute confidence in her helping spirits. We were also graced with the presence of Professor Mongush Kenin-Lopsan, recognized by the Foundation for Shamanic Studies as a Living Treasure of Shamanism and a renowned scholar. Living Treasures are indigenous shamans who receive financial help from the FSS. His gentle presence belied the courage he showed for many years as he preserved shamanic knowledge in the face of the Soviet persecution of shamans. I attended a party held in Saratoga, CA for the Tuvans after the training ended. They were presented with gifts, for which they expressed genuine gratitude. A strong memory of that evening was their insistence on saving the gift wrapping paper. Paper, we were told, is at a premium in distant Tuva. With the presence on the altar of the card depicting a Tuvan lake, I am reminded of the great home of shamanism, Siberia;

of the wonderful Tuvans whose visit I will always remember; and of the fact that the Earth abounds in great beauty.

8 | THE MALA

While writing this book, I decided to add a new item to the altar: a set of mala beads. Recently, my wife Shana and I attended a modified Kharga Puja healing ceremony in Alexandria, VA, organized by a good friend and spiritual sister, and lead by a Nepalese shaman (or jhankri), Bhola nath Banstola. The ceremony allows a group of people to release old wounds and receive healing from the spirits. Bhola is a very kind and gentle man, seemingly tireless, with a youthful demeanor. He always seems to be smiling. When one is in his presence, one feels accepted and appreciated. At the end of the ceremony, he presented Shana and me with a mala (a set of beads used in certain meditation practices).

Bhola reminds me of another extraordinary person, Brother David Steindl-Rast, a Benedictine monk based in Switzerland, who travels extensively around the world bridging the gaps between different spiritualities. I first saw Brother David at Esalen Institute in the mid-80s and never forgot him. There is an aura about him that draws people to him. He is closely associated with the website www.Gratefulness.org. Gratefulness is a major theme of his teachings. I met him officially in

January 2013 at the Foundation for Shamanic Studies annual Council Meeting, where he and Michael Harner engaged in a dialogue on stage in front of an audience. Brother David mentioned the similarities between the Christian idea of the risen Christ and the Buddhist concept of the Rainbow Body. Sogyal Rinpoche, in *The Tibetan Book of Living and Dying*, discusses the Rainbow Body:

> *Through these advanced practices of Dzogchen, accomplished practitioners can bring their lives to an extraordinary and triumphant end. As they die, they enable their body to be reabsorbed back into the light essence of the elements that created it, and consequently their material body dissolves into light and then disappears completely. This process is known as the 'rainbow body' or 'body of light,' because the dissolution is often accompanied by spontaneous manifestations of light and rainbows.*

Shana and I introduced ourselves to Brother David, and after shaking hands, he bowed to us touching his forehead to our hands, an unforgettable gesture of humility.

As I think of the mala, I am taken back to a time in the late '70's, when several of my acquaintances were wearing malas. These acquaintances were devotees of Bhagwan Shree Rajneesh, the Indian guru later known as Osho, the Golden Guru. I had read a number of Rajneesh's books—some of them were explanations of various spiritual paths. Sometimes called the "Sex

Guru," Osho emphasized the importance of freedom, love and meditation. His writings inspired me to visit the Rajneesh Meditation Center in Washington DC in 1979. It was an unforgettable day. I met with the 'swamis' or 'sannyasins' living at the center, devoted followers of their guru. These were down-to-earth people, mostly African-American men, at this particular center. Swami Deben was particularly kind and knowledgeable.

Scheduled for the afternoon was Osho's renowned Dynamic Meditation. He had devised a number of powerful and often highly physical meditations. The Dynamic is comprised of five parts: chaotic breathing, let-go, the aerobic jumping "whoo" phase, the "freeze" phase, and finally the celebratory free flowing movement phase. Invited to join the sannyasins in the Dynamic, I had no idea of what I was getting myself into. We performed the meditation in the basement of the ashram. During the "let-go" phase, I was certain I was in the midst of madmen, some of whom were howling, others screaming, others crying. Tempted to quickly leave and head home, I hung in and completed all of the phases of this remarkable meditation. Lying down in the darkness afterwards, I had a vision of golden light flowing down from the heavens into the room and into my body. I had experienced, as far as I knew, my first vision, and this without the aid of psychoactive substances. I spent many an evening and afternoon with the "orange people" (devotees wore orange, red, or purple clothing), hanging out and doing a variety of meditations. Although Osho died in 1990, his work is very much alive today. There is the main ashram in Poona, India; a large number of his books are in print; and CDs that accompany his meditations are readily available. We did meditations for thirty days in a row once. I have never felt better than I did after that month of altered state experience.

It was during this time that I learned about a workshop being held in Luray, VA, featuring an anthropologist and expert in shamanism named Michael Harner, author of *The Way of the Shaman*, whom I have already mentioned frequently throughout this book. The Basic Workshop that took place in October, 1981 is still fresh in my memory. Michael showed us how to experience visions easily with the assistance of the drum. Beyond that, he introduced the world of spirits to us, enabling us to find and utilize the help of spiritual allies that are altogether real. The rest is history, as the saying goes. Eventually, I threw myself into shamanism and the instruction of Dr. Harner, another remarkable person who has deeply influenced my life. Despite his vast knowledge and experience, Michael has often reminded us that "the spirits are the real experts."

I associate the mala with one other major influence in my life—Rudy Bauer, Ph.D., clinical psychologist and Co-Director of the Washington Center for Consciousness Studies.[3] I have spent much time with Rudy over the last 22 years. Rudy has made a long study of different spiritual practices and spent a

---

3   http://www.meditatelive.com

number of years as a student of the well-known Swami Muktananda. Fraternizing with a genius like Rudy with his tremendous insights into human behavior and spirituality has offered me an opportunity to mature, develop and become a much freer person. Rudy indirectly taught me how to better work with groups of people. He continues to be a source of wisdom and light.

9 | THE ROUTE 66 MEDALLION

There is a place, a road actually, which is also a state of mind, a dream, and a symbol. It is called Route 66, The Mother Road, and it once ran from Chicago, IL to Santa Monica, CA. This was one of the great highways of the United States and, until replaced by the Interstate Highway System, was one of the main thoroughfares in the United States running east-west. It was a major route for those escaping the Dust Bowl of the 30s and served as a focus for commerce for decades beginning in 1926 until it was officially dropped from the U.S. highway system in 1985. Many portions of the road remain and there have been major efforts to preserve motels, neon signs, gas stations, and other historic features along the road.

Being the family of a U.S. Army officer meant that when I was young we were nomads, never spending more than three years in any one place. Consequently, we traveled the pre-interstate roads of America in the late 40s, the 50s, and early 60s. Our travels took us to California, New Jersey, New Orleans, Long Island, Tidewater, VA, Washington, DC and places in between; to post-World War II Frankfurt, Germany in 1949 where my playgrounds were bombed out buildings; and to the Azores Islands, where some inhabitants seemed to be living as their ancestors did 300 years before.

Bruce Chatwin wrote a lovely book titled *The Songlines,* named after the trails that Australian aborigines follow retracing the paths of the 'Dreamtime Beings.' Chatwin strongly suggests that the natural lifestyle of humanity is that of the nomad. This may be true, but it doesn't prevent the pain and discomfort of regularly saying goodbye to fellow nomads or those we know who have settled in one place. Many 'moderns' have indeed adopted lifestyles or jobs that honor humanity's wanderlust identified in *The Songlines.* One of the beauties of the shamanic journey is that we can satisfy our penchant for travel through spiritual means. There seem to be an infinite number of places/ environments/creatures/people available to us in the spirit worlds. As we look at ourselves and our impact on the planet, we might ask ourselves how our species lost its way—for surely this is the case. Perhaps we didn't know that there literally was a 'way,' in fact many ways, and we were meant to travel them physically and/ or spiritually.

After returning to the U.S. in the summer of 1961, I spent a couple of months with my uncle and his family in Riverhead, Long Island, NY. A strong and pleasant memory is our sitting together watching the television series *Route 66* on Friday nights. Possessing one of the great theme songs of all time and filmed on location across the U.S., the fictional program depicted the adventures of buddies Todd and Buz (played by a couple of great actors and two of my favorite famous people, Martin Milner and George Maharis) as they motored from place to place in their Chevrolet Corvette, encountering people and situations brought to life by some of television's best-ever scripts. Their life of adventure, as they sought a place they could call home, became my dream.

Television, in its relative infancy, had many redeeming qualities. In *Route 66*, two young men with tremendous compassion traveled in search of their Holy Grail, embodying decency, honor and strength in the midst of ignorance, violence, and helplessness. This program and certain others from the 50s and 60s presented viewers with an unspoken code of honor that influenced me and, no doubt, many others. A few years later Crosby, Stills, Nash and Young would sing, "You, who are on the road, must have a code that you can live by." Todd and Buz had a code as they explored places, people, and ways of making a living. In my career as a workshop facilitator, I have traveled extensively, and I have in fact continued the pattern of movement established early in my life. Over the years and through what at the time I construed to be mistakes, I have developed a simple code I remind myself of regularly: do the right thing and use common sense. This applies to everyday life, and it applies to shamanic work.

Granted, "the right thing" and "common sense" are somewhat ambiguous concepts, and they vary from person to person and culture to culture. The salient point is that I usually understand what they mean for me and that in adhering to them, I am impacting the world in a positive way. Perhaps this must be the focus of humanity now: to be the most positive force possible. After all, don't we owe a debt to our planet, to the land, the air and the sea? As the Eskimos say in speaking of the ocean, but what can also be applied to the planet as a whole, "She makes us glad, she feeds us, she makes us glad, she feeds us, and every living thing near here she feeds."

The Route 66 medallion on the altar, another new addition, reminds me of the wind and the currents of the sea flowing to places undiscovered. It speaks of freedom of thought, freedom of movement, freedom to be true to oneself; freedom from the shackles of cultural conditioning, from the confines of materialism, from the limitations of conformity. It is therefore an embodiment of the spirit of Michael Harner's core shamanism which tells us that we all can have our own unique relationship with the spirits and their worlds. In the end, the medallion and the things it represents remind me of our planet's miraculous birds, the descendants of the great dinosaurs. As the great John Lennon once wrote, "Free, as a bird, it's the next best thing to be, free as a bird."

CLOSING THOUGHTS

Once again, as I said at the beginning of this book, I do not call myself a shaman. I aspire to being the eternal student and to remembering the teachings of the Great Ones with whom I have come into significant contact. I have no desire to be anyone but myself. In not attaching too much importance to myself, I hope to be like a feather, surrendering to the winds of opportunity and perhaps even fate, solid in its own way and perfectly designed for movement.

I encourage all readers to build an altar that honors their teachers, allies, and loved ones, to give it thought, and to visit it regularly. I hope that readers will consider what it means to be alive and to think of what it takes to be a responsible and unique human being; that people everywhere will treat animals and plants with the utmost respect. Finally, I hope that readers will contemplate what freedom entails, how one can achieve freedom of thought and freedom of action, and finally discover the way to beauty and truth.

BIBLIOGRAPHY

Bakker, Robert. *The Dinosaur Heresies*. New York: Kensington, 1996.

Bates, Brian. *The Way of the Actor*. Boston: Shambhala, 1988.

Brodzky, Anne. *Stones, Bones and Skin*. Toronto: The Society for Art, 1977.

Chatwin, Bruce. *The Songlines*. New York: Penguin Books, 1987.

Cowan, Tom. *Fire in the Head*. San Francisco: Harper Collins, 1993.

Crosby, Stills, Nash and Young. "Teach Your Children Well" in *Déjà Vu*. Atlantic Records, 1970. Compact disc.

Gaup, Ailo. *In Search of the Drum*. Fort Yates: Muse, 1993.

Gordon, James. *The Golden Guru*. New York: Penguin, 1988.

Harner, Michael. *Cave and Cosmos*. Berkeley: North Atlantic Books, 2012.

Harner, Michael. *The Jivaro*. Berkeley: University of California, 1972.

Harner, Michael. *The Way of the Shaman*. San Francisco: Harper Collins, 1990.

Hunt, Norman. *Shamanism in North America*. Buffalo: Firefly, 2002.

Lamb, F. Bruce. *The Wizard of the Upper Amazon*. Berkeley: North Atlantic Books, 1974.

Lennon, John, et al. "Free As a Bird" in the Beatles' *Anthology 1*. Capitol, 1995. Compact disc.

Linn, Denise. *Altars*. Ballantine: New York, 1999.

MacDonald, John D. *Condominium*. New York: Fawcett, 1977.

MacDonald, John D. *The Damned*. Greenwich: Fawcett, 1952.

MacDonald, John D. *A Deadly Shade of Gold*. New York: Ballantine, 1995.

MacDonald, John D. *A Flash of Green*. New York: Ballantine, 1983.

MacDonald, John D. *A Friendship*. New York: Knopf, 1986.

MacDonald, John D. and Kilpack, Capt. John. *Nothing Can Go Wrong*. New York: Ballantine, 1982.

MacDonald, John D. *Please Write for Details*. Greenwich: Fawcett, 1959.

Mails, Thomas. *Plains Indians*. New York: Bonanza, 1985.

Mitchell, Joni. "Woodstock" in *Ladies of the Canyon*. Warner Bros.,1990. Compact disc.

Random House Webster's College Dictionary. New York: Random House, 1991. Print.

Rinpoche, Sogyal. *The Tibetan Book of Living and Dying.* San Francisco: Harper Collins, 1992.

Roberts, Jane. *The Nature of Personal Reality.* San Rafael: Amber-Allen, 1994.

Roberts, Jane. *Seth Speaks.* San Rafael: Amber-Allen, 1994.

Route 66, Prod. Stirling Silliphant. CBS. WCBS, New York City. 1961. Television.

Sarangerel. *Chosen by the Spirits.* Rochester, VT: Destiny, 2001.

Tkacz, Virlana. *Shanar.* New York: Parabola, 2002.

Tourtellot, Jonathan B. National Park Destinations Rated." *National Geographic Traveler*, July/August, 2005.

Wolfen, Dir. Michael Wadleigh, Orion Pictures, 1981.

Web Sites

http://www.Gratefulness.org. Gratefulness.org, September 1, 2013.

http://www.indianpueblo.org/19pueblos/zia.htm. Zia Pueblo, September 1, 2013.

http://www.meditatelive.com. Washington Center for Consciousness Studies, September 1, 2013.

http://www.nepalese.it/en/bholadocs/01. Nepalese Shamanism for Peace and Brotherhood, September 1, 2013.

http://www.shamanism.org/articles/article08.html.
Foundation for Shamanic Studies, September 1,
2013.

http://shamanism.org/fssinfo/livingtreasureKenin-
Lopsan.html. Foundation for Shamanic Studies,
September 1, 2013.

http://www.utexas.edu/courses/sami/diehtu/giella/
music/yoiksunna.htm. Sami Culture, September 1,
2013.

http://www.utexas.edu/courses/sami/diehtu/siida/
hunting/jonsa.htm. Sami Culture, September 1,
2013.

Resources

Dana's website: www.shamantracks.com

The Foundation for Shamanic Studies:
www.shamanism.org

Washington Center for Consciousness Studies:
http://www.meditatelive.com

Save the Manatee Club: www.savethemanatee.org

Ralph Aragon (rattles, pottery, shields): 013 Northeast
Drive, Zia Pueblo, NM 87053

Lightning Source UK Ltd.
Milton Keynes UK
UKHW010605011222
413111UK00013B/2564

9 780990 350057